KU-166-283

I SEE SCIENCE

LIGHT

DISCOVER THE SCIENCE ALL AROUND YOU

IZZI HOWELL

WAYLAND

First published in Great Britain in 2022 by Wayland
Copyright © Hodder and Stoughton, 2022

Produced for Wayland by
White-Thomson Publishing Ltd
www.wtpub.co.uk

All rights reserved
HB 978 1 5263 1502 1
PB 978 1 5263 1508 3

Editor: Izzi Howell
Designer: Clare Nicholas
All illustrations by Christos Skaltsas
All design elements from Shutterstock, including 13c 0merta

Printed in Dubai

Wayland
An imprint of
Hachette Children's Group
Part of Hodder and Stoughton
Carmelite House
50 Victoria Embankment
London EC4Y 0DZ

An Hachette UK Company
www.hachette.co.uk
www.hachettechildrens.co.uk

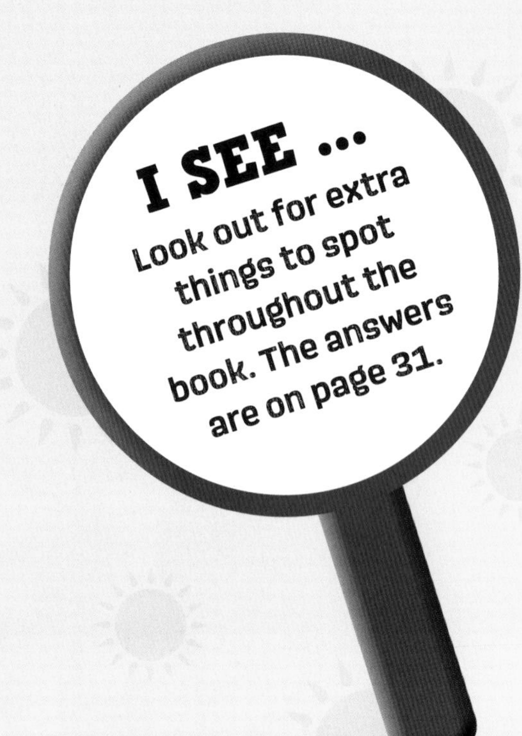

CONTENTS

LIGHT

Light is a type of energy.
It allows us to see things.

The Sun shines during the day.

At night, we have to use electric lights.

Light is important for all living things.

Light can pass through some materials.

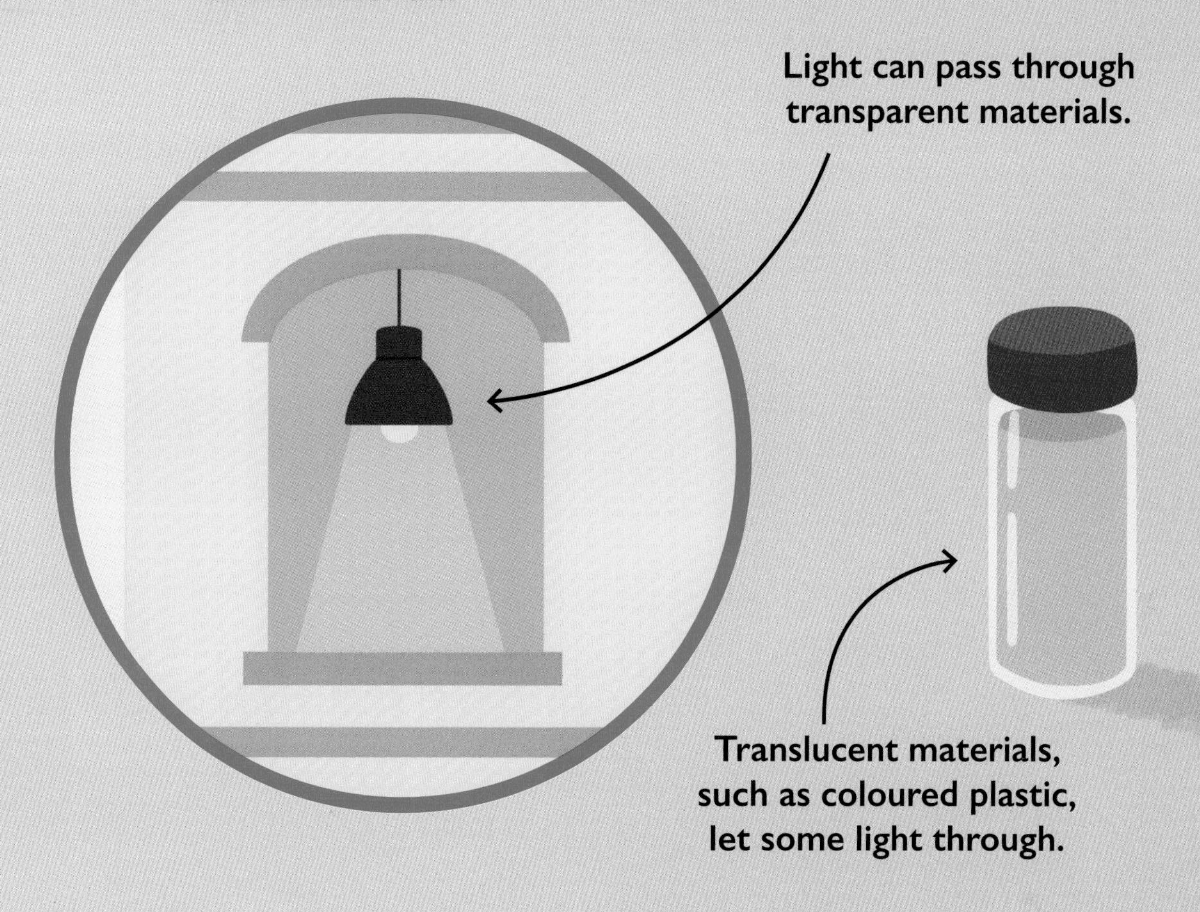

Light can pass through transparent materials.

Translucent materials, such as coloured plastic, let some light through.

Light can't pass through opaque materials.

DAY AND NIGHT

Light sources produce light.

The Moon looks like it is shining, but it is actually reflecting light from the Sun.
Flames from candles produce light.
We can also use electric lights when it's dark outside.

ALL ABOUT LIGHT SOURCES

Some light sources are natural. Others are made by humans.

The Sun is the biggest source of natural light on Earth. It is a massive star at the centre of our solar system.

The Sun's rays can be dangerous. You should never look directly at the Sun because it will hurt your eyes. The Sun can also burn your skin, so you should cover up and wear suncream.

Electric lights are a human-made light source. They are powered by electricity so you can use them at any time of day.

Fire and flames are natural sources of light. In the past, people used candles to see at night because they didn't have electric lights.

The Moon shines brightly in the night sky, but it isn't a light source. It actually reflects light from the Sun.

Other stars are light sources, but they are too far away for us to use the light they produce.

I SEE ...

Can you see another natural light source on page 7?

LIGHT AND SIGHT

We see objects when light reflects off them or if they give off light.

Light travels from a light source to an object.

Light reflects off objects and travels into our eyes.

The brain
understands what
you are looking at.
The eyes send a
signal to the brain.
Light moves in
straight lines.

ALL ABOUT SEEING THINGS

Light, eyes and the brain work together to allow you to see.

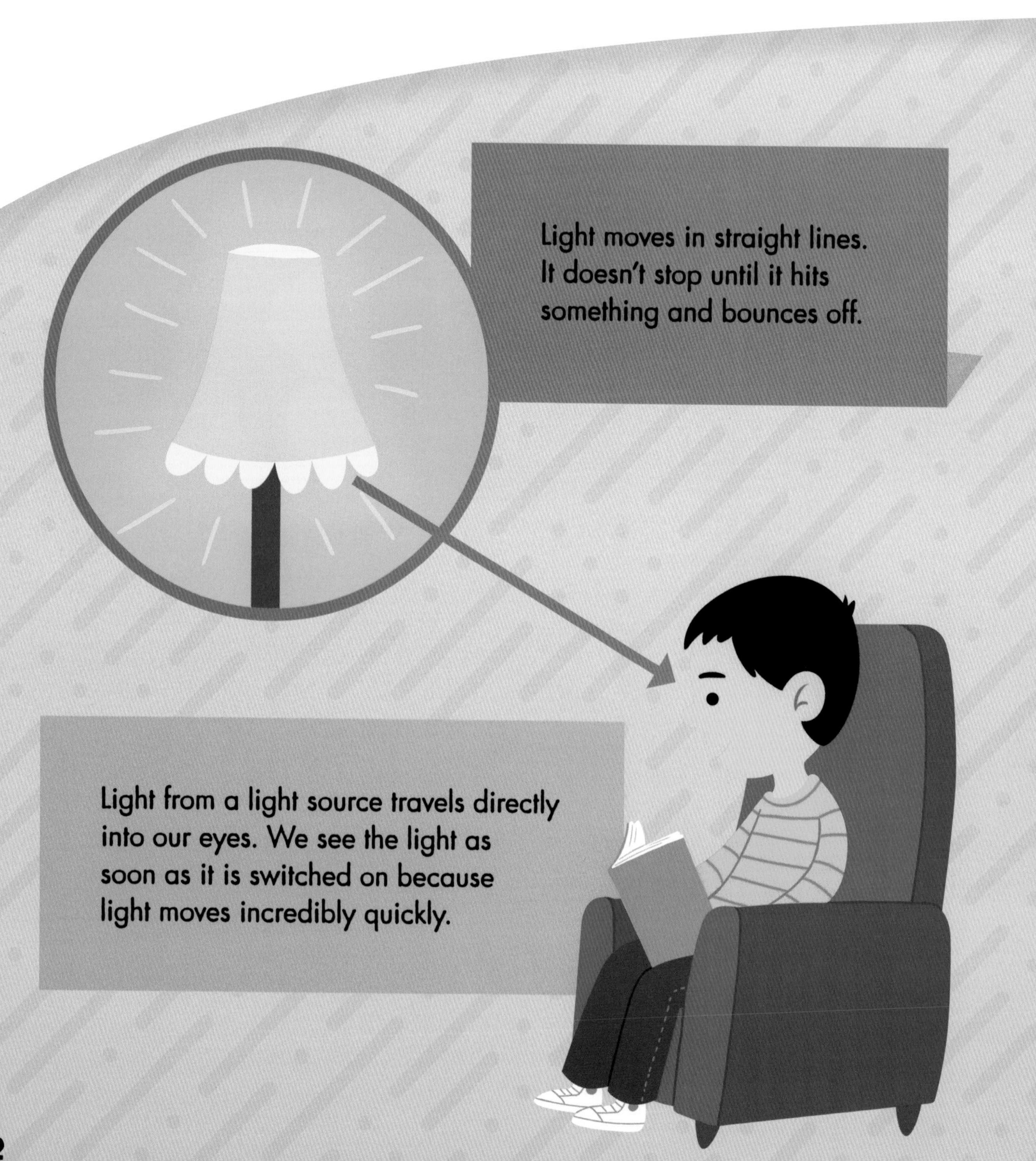

We see objects that aren't light sources when light reflects off them. The reflected light travels into our eyes.

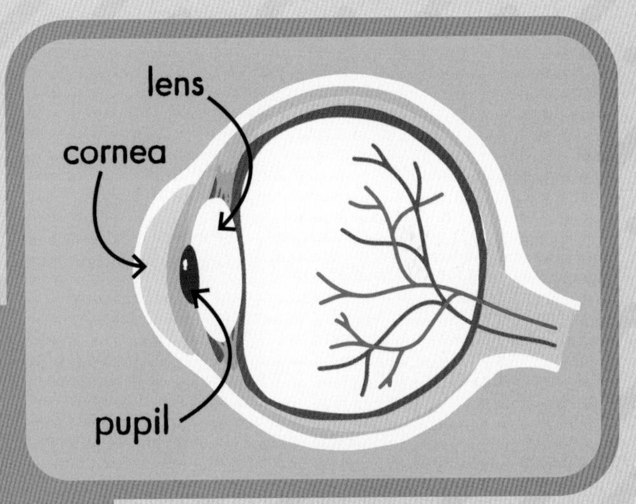

The eye is very sensitive. There are many different parts that work together to allow us to see.

We wouldn't be able to see anything at all without the brain. The brain understands signals from the eyes and turns them into the images that we see.

I SEE ...

Can you see some more eyes on page 10?

REFLECTING LIGHT

Light changes direction when it hits an object.

Shiny, smooth surfaces reflect light well.

Dark, dull surfaces don't reflect light well.

When light hits an uneven surface, the light is scattered.

When light hits a flat surface, it reflects back at the same angle.
A shiny, flat mirror creates a clear reflection.
A reflection in water can look distorted.

ALL ABOUT REFLECTIONS

When light bounces off a shiny object, we see a reflection.

Smooth, shiny surfaces create even reflections. We can see a clear image reflected back.

The reflection you see in a mirror is exactly the same as the object, but reversed. Something on the left in real life will appear on the right in a mirror.

Dark, dull surfaces absorb nearly all of the light rays, so no reflection can be seen.

Uneven, shiny surfaces, such as water with ripples, create distorted reflections. This is because the light bounces off the surface at different angles.

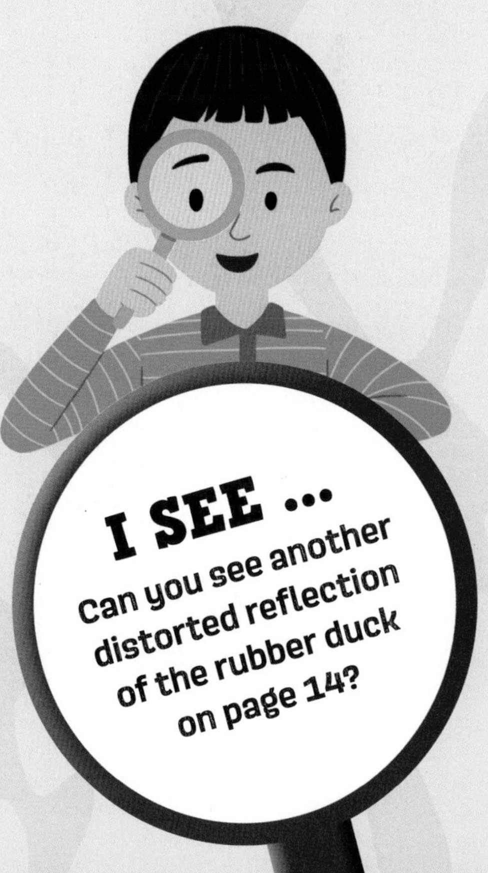

BLOCKING LIGHT

When an opaque object blocks light, it creates a shadow.

There is no light on the other side of the object. This dark area is called a shadow.

Shadows can look like the object blocking the light.

Light can't travel through opaque objects.

Shadows change shape depending on the position of the light source.
Translucent objects can also form shadows as they block some light too.
Shadows change size depending on the distance from the light source.

ALL ABOUT SHADOWS

Shadows change when a light source gets closer or changes position.

The Sun is the only light source hitting this play structure, so it only has one shadow. However, if two light sources were shining on it, it would have two shadows!

If you move, your shadow moves with you! This is because you block a new section of light when you move.

The closer an object is to a light source, the bigger its shadow. If an object is far away from a light, it will have a smaller shadow.

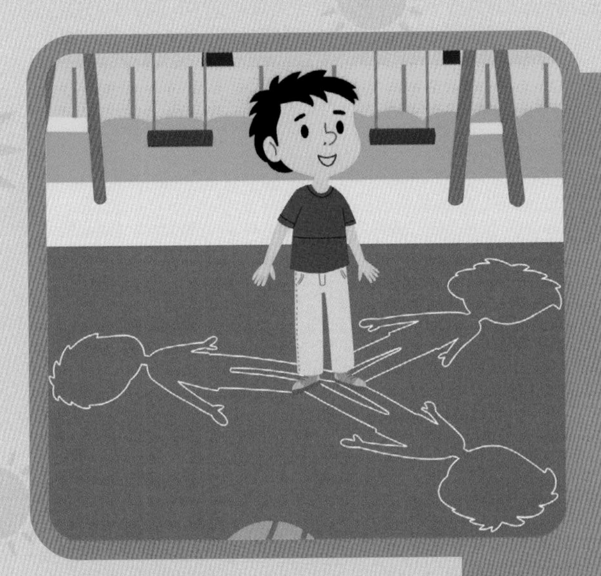

If the position of a light source changes, shadows change too. Outdoor shadows change size throughout the day because the Sun moves across the sky. You can test this out by tracing the outline of your shadow in chalk at different times of day.

Translucent objects form shadows because they let some light pass through. However, their shadows are weaker than those created by opaque objects.

COLOURED LIGHT

We see objects as different colours because of the way they reflect and absorb light.

Light looks white but it is made up of many different colours.

Dark objects absorb all the colours of light.

A yellow object reflects yellow light and absorbs all other colours of light.

The sky looks blue
even though air
is colourless!
A rainbow is made up of
different colours of light.
White objects reflect
all the colours of light
that hit them.

ALL ABOUT COLOUR

Coloured objects reflect different colours of light.

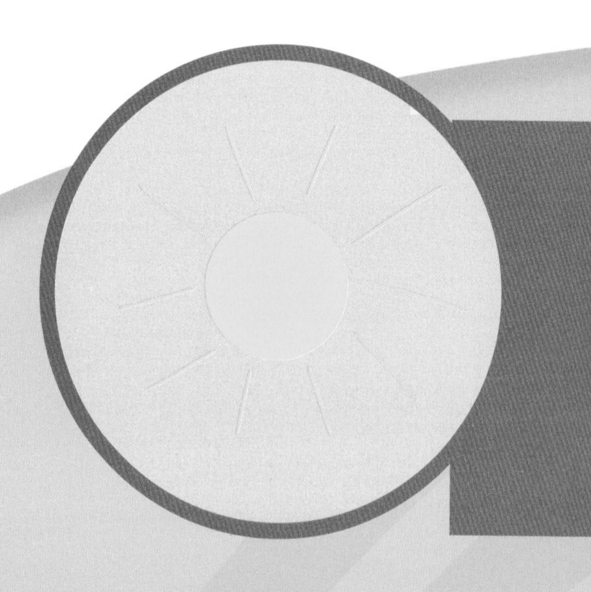

White light is made up of many different colours of light, such as red light, yellow light and blue light. However, we can't usually see all of the different colours.

When light hits a coloured object, such as a yellow coat, the coat absorbs all the other colours of light except yellow. The yellow light is reflected into our eyes, and we see the coat as yellow.

When light hits a white object, all of the colours of light are reflected into our eyes. The different colours of light combine together to make white light, and we see the object as white.

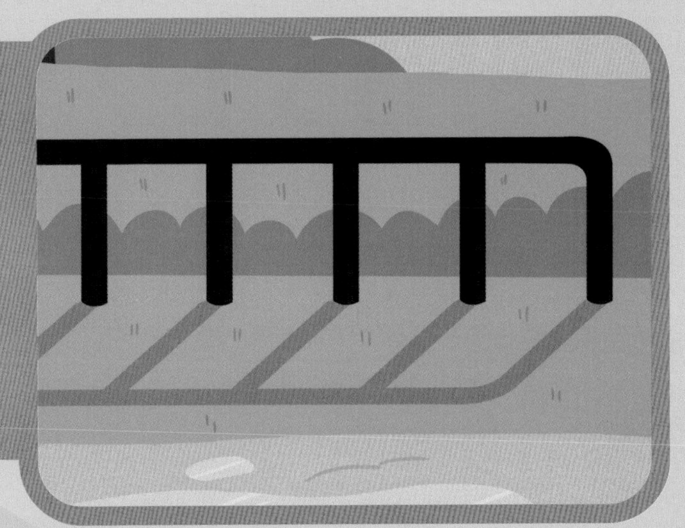

When light hits a dark object, its surface absorbs all of the colours of light. No coloured light is reflected into our eyes, and the object appears dark.

A rainbow forms when light hits raindrops in the sky. The raindrops split the light into many different colours.

Sunlight is split into different colours of light in the air. The rays of blue light are smaller and shorter than those of other colours, which makes them easiest for us to see. This is why the sky looks blue!

LIGHTS EVERYWHERE

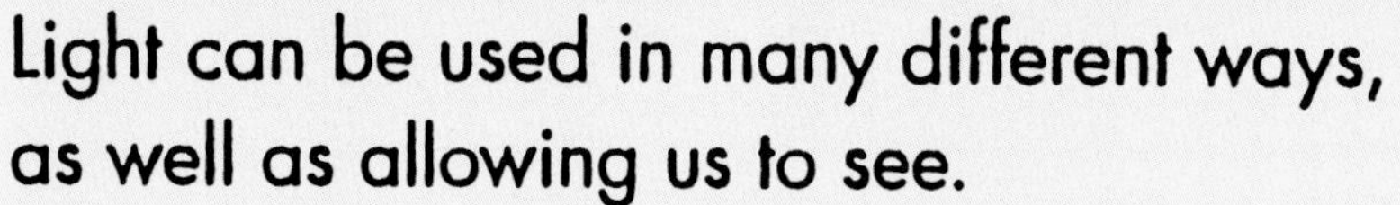

Light can be used in many different ways, as well as allowing us to see.

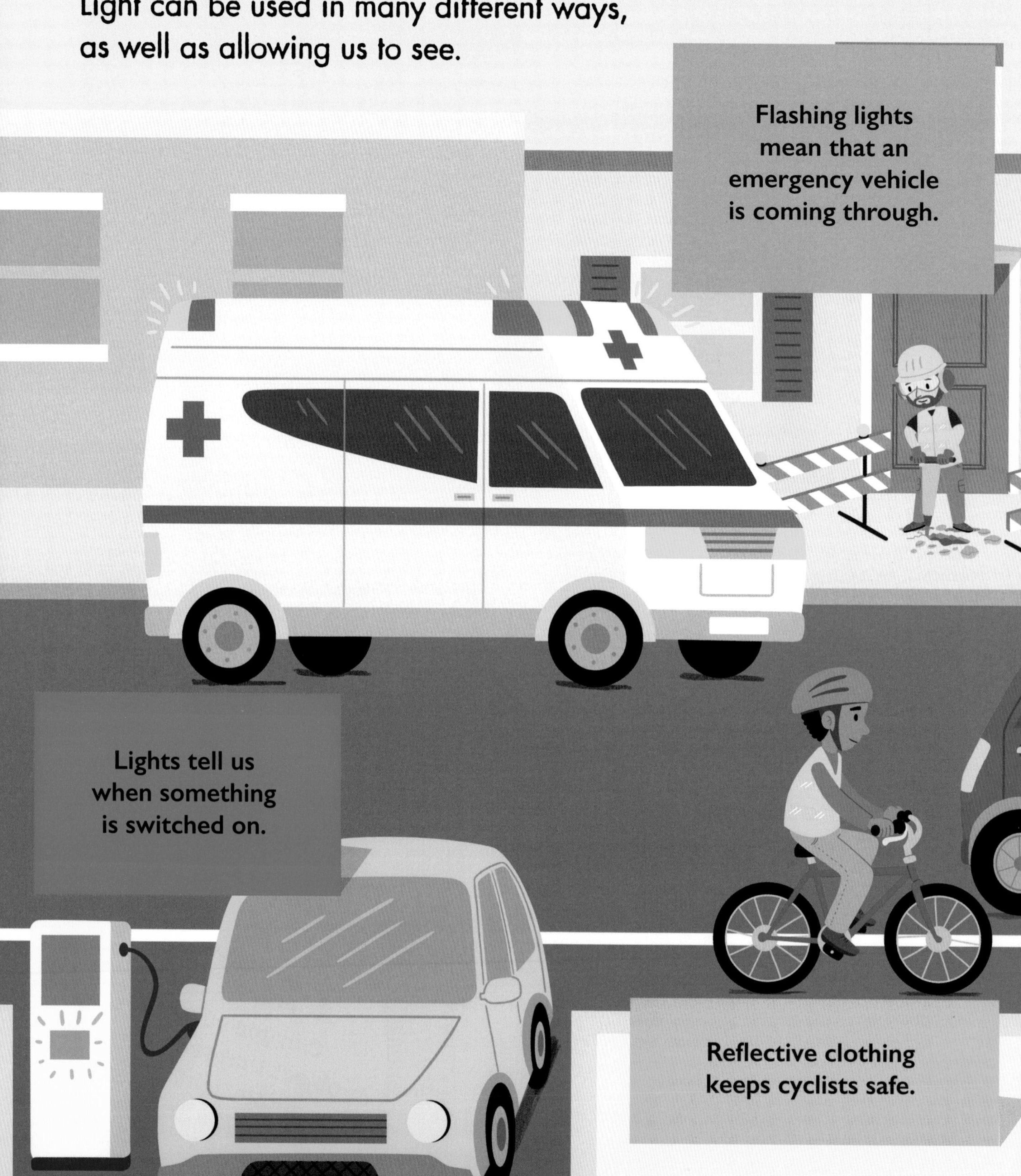

A red pedestrian crossing light means that you need to wait to cross the road.
Plants make their own food using sunlight.
A green traffic light means that vehicles can go.

ALL ABOUT USING LIGHT

Light can be used to make food for plants, keep people safe and show us if machines are switched on.

Plants need sunlight to grow and stay healthy. During the day, plants turn sunlight into food in their leaves. This process is called photosynthesis.

Reflective clothing keeps cyclists and other people safe around roads. Light reflects off the clothing and helps drivers to see them.

We use different colours of light to tell people and vehicles when to move. Red means stop, amber (orangey yellow) means get ready to go, and green means go!

Bright, flashing lights are used to get our attention. Emergency vehicles have flashing lights so other drivers know to let them pass. These lights can also show that a machine isn't working properly.

Many electric appliances use lights to show that they are plugged in or switched on. This lets us know that they are working.

GLOSSARY

absorb – to take something in

angle – the position of something

appliance – a machine or piece of equipment, often used in the home, such as a washing machine

distorted – pulled or twisted out of shape

dull – not shiny

human-made – describes something that has been made by people

light source – something that gives off light

natural – describes something that is found in nature and was not made by humans

opaque – describes something that does not let light through

reflect – if an object reflects light, light bounces off it and is not absorbed

reflective – describes something that sends back most of the light that shines on it

reversed – the opposite way round

shadow – an area of darkness caused by something blocking light

translucent – describes something that some light can pass through

transparent – describes something that you can see through

uneven – not flat or smooth

ANSWERS

page 9: lightning

page 13: the photographs on the shelf

page 17: the duck reflected in the bath tap

page 21: the rabbit shadow on the wall of the play structure

page 25: an umbrella

page 29: a construction worker

FURTHER INFORMATION

BOOKS

Investigating Light (Be a Scientist) by Jacqui Bailey, Wayland, 2020

Light (Boom Science) by Georgia Amson-Bradshaw, Wayland, 2019

Light (Discover and Do) by Jane Lacey, Franklin Watts, 2021

Light (Quick Fix Science) by Paul Mason, Wayland, 2021

WEBSITES

www.bbc.co.uk/bitesize/clips/z7bmyrd

Watch a video about shadows and the Sun.

www.educationquizzes.com/ks2/science/shadows-and-reflections

Take a quiz about shadows and reflection.

www.dkfindout.com/uk/science/light

Find out more about light and reflections.

INDEX

I SEE SCIENCE

Titles in the series

Forces and magnets
Forces everywhere
All about forces
Slide and stop
All about friction
Moving through
All about resistance
Up and down
All about gravity
Studying magnets
All about magnets
Magnets around the house
All about using magnets

Light
Day and night
All about light sources
Light and sight
All about seeing things
Reflecting light
All about reflections
Blocking light
All about shadows
Coloured light
All about colours
Lights everywhere
All about using light

Living things
A world of animals
All about animals
New life begins
All about life cycles
Plants everywhere
All about plants
A seashore habitat
All about habitats
Habitats through the year
All about seasons
Who eats whom?
All about food chains

Materials
A world of materials
All about properties
Choosing the right material
All about testing materials
Shape and state
All about changing materials
Making materials
All about natural and human-made materials
Electricity on the move
All about electricity
Keeping warm
All about heat

Sound
Rise and shine
All about sound waves
Hearing sounds
All about the ear
Sound on the street
All about volume
High and low
All about pitch
Bouncing back
All about echoes
Playing music
All about musical instruments

States of matter
Spotting solids
All about solids
Fill it up
All about liquids
Blow to inflate
All about gases
Hot and cold
All about melting and freezing
Wet and dry
All about boiling, evaporation and condensation
Rain to river
All about the water cycle